POCKET BOOK OF PUNS – PARDON?

Kimi Cowie-McCash

Follow me on twitter @poppyscot

Whiteboards are remarkable.

I made a chicken salad and the ungrateful sod never ate it.

To neigh or not to neigh? That is equestrian.

Hedgehogs: Why can't they be nice and share the hedge?

I saw 'Titanic' in 3D. The person in 4D asked me to take my hat off.

I work as a waiter. The pay is awful but at least I can put food on the table.

I can't stand French jokes. They are crepe.

Follow me on twitter @poppyscot

Have you noticed that people lean forward slightly when they nod their head? I must admit I'm inclined to agree with them.

I wore an outfit of mirrors today. I'm at the age when I do a lot of reflecting.

Follow me on twitter @poppyscot

“This is my step, mum” “Very nice honey but why did you build one?”

I gave up my job as an origami teacher. There was far too much paperwork.

My friends call me weird because I swallowed an abacus. They don’t realise it what’s on the inside that counts.

It bugs the life out of me when people use insects in their jokes.

I’ve said it before and I’ll say it again; there is nothing more annoying than people who repeat themselves.

Meeting: a place where minutes are taken but hours are wasted.

Follow me on twitter @poppyscot

I gave my friend my copy of Office XP but she didn't want anyone to know. She has my word.

I have a new job working at the Royal Mint. I am shocked at how much money I make!

Follow me on twitter @poppyscot

Why did the Mafia cross the road? For revenge – the road had crossed him earlier.

I created an upside down house and it's now a top cellar.

If I find myself down in the dumps I get a coat to cheer myself up. They do smell a lot but they are free.

I can't remember the last time I heard a pun about boats. Canoe?

Support your local search and rescue squad: get lost.

I had a candlelit dinner last night. The food was still raw.

Follow me on twitter @poppyscot

I bought a flea circus yesterday but one won't be fired out of the cannon. He's a nervous tick.

Follow me on twitter @poppyscot

The French make omelettes with one egg as in France one is an ouef.

My grandmother slipped on some beans last week. If only she had Heinz sight.

My friend is a photographer and he is always depressed. I think he focuses on the negatives too much.

The 'Invisible Man' married the 'Invisible Woman'. Their kids were nothing to look at either.

My friend is fascinated by magnets. Personally, I don't see the attraction.

I bought a second hand 'Jack in the box' but it's useless. It doesn't surprise me.

You won't believe me when I tell you I'm a big liar.

Follow me on twitter @poppyscot

A fisherman decided to learn the alphabet but unfortunately he got lost at C.

It pains me to say it but I've got a sore throat.

You know you're getting old when your narrow waist swaps places with your broad mind.

Follow me on twitter @poppyscot

Nothing quite says 'Loser' more than having a tattoo saying 'Loser' across your forehead.

For the record, I bought a vinyl cleaning kit.

Understanding the horizon is way beyond me.

If I meet a pretty girl I always look out for signs of intelligence. If she doesn't show any then we'll get along great.

I couldn't believe the world came crashing down around me the other day. I found some blue tac and put it back up.

I am really big in China. I'm 6ft 2.

My wife closed the lid on the piano. I can't get into it now as the keys are on the inside.

Follow me on twitter @poppyscot

A good pun has its own reword.

I've always asked too many questions? Does anyone have any idea why?

Too cut a long story short get some scissors.

When I die, I'm going to attend every concert I want for free

I wonder what the sign for 'dot' is in Braille?

Noticed this sign in our local camping shop 'This is the discount of our winter tent'.

If you are ever trying to talk your way out of a speeding ticket, I find confessing to murder works.

At customs I was asked to step into a room for a cavity search. Why on earth would I struggle drugs through in my teeth?

I've lost the plot. I keep ripping pages out of my book.

All my time at the gym is paying off. I managed to stop a taxi with one hand today.

Looking after my child is going to be expensive. I've just had to buy a baby monitor, for crying out loud.

Follow me on twitter @poppyscot

I met Steve Davis was at an exhibition show recently. He invited me to pick a pocket so I stole his chalk.

An Italian man started throwing dough, cheese and tomatoes at me. I asked him "Do you want a pizza me?"

Do deaf mathematicians speak in sine language?

What do you call a baby sheep between two sheets of plastic? Lambinated.

I have a Scottish lady who decorates my bathroom for me. Her name is Bonnie Tiler.

I have dressed up as a knife for a fancy dress party. I think I look very sharp.

Follow me on twitter @poppyscot

I don't like blowing my own trumpet which is why I was asked to leave the orchestra.

Every street I walk down has at least one rubbish bin. You would think they would try to replace them with nicer ones.

Always listen to the pen. It has a point.

DFS Sale: 'Don't pay any interest' – okay when I'm looking for a sofa I'll walk past your shop and turn my head away.

Beauty is in the eye of the beer holder.

Follow me on twitter @poppyscot

I heard a Mime artist was strangled with a cordless phone the other day.

I had an out of body experience earlier; I was beside myself.

Does any one else think that pregnancy lasts a maternity?

Follow me on twitter @poppyscot

I went into hospital for surgery. Surgery being the operative word.

After putting weight on I was sacked from my job as a Donald Duck impersonator. Seemingly I no longer fitted the bill.

I'm multi national. I'm part Scottish and part Welsh. Scottish on my mother's side and welsh on my father's friends' side.

Safety in numbers? When I joined the lunchtime mathematics society I got bullied even more.

I was talking to my cat the other day and we both think you are crazy.

I continue to help the Scottish Economy by buying a bottle of whisky a day.

Follow me on twitter @poppyscot

Breasts are the paper weights of the soul.

Me? A sceptic? I hope you have proof.

I always avoid fighting on the moving stairs as I find it can escalate every easily.

I was arrested for running down the naked spraying deodorant. I can't help acting on Impulse.

Follow me on twitter @poppyscot

I have a theory that it's impossible to prove anything. But I can't prove it.

Thanks to the metric system an inchworm can become a caterpillar.

It has taken me years to perfect the invisible coat. All I have to do now is remember where I left it.

If you were left along on a desert island what one luxury would you take with you? A boat.

My mate offered me things that he had stolen off the back of a lorry. Quite what I could do with a large door and a registration plate is beyond me.

I always find I'm in the right place at the right time. Just so happens to be on the wrong day.

Follow me on twitter @poppyscot

I just poured super glue into a non stick pot.

Someone is about to be proven wrong.

What's worse than finding a spider in your bedroom late at night? Losing a spider in your bedroom late at night.

A facial tattoo is a perfect way to say "I don't care what you think."

Follow me on twitter @poppyscot

Why isn't phonetic spelt the way it sounds?

I've been looking into observational comedy recently.

Have you noticed how hard it is to make a comeback when you've never gone anywhere?

Follow me on twitter @poppyscot

I used to work upstairs in a clock factory. I always had to work overtime.

I've just watched a person fall over in the street. I laughed but must admit it wasn't the same without background music.

My friend bought a parrot recently. I think that says a lot about her.

I have loads of books on the Supernatural, Ghosts and Crop Circles. I didn't buy them, they just appeared.

I always wanted to be a taxi driver as they are really popular. I always see people waving at them.

They say that history repeats itself but they've said that before.

Follow me on twitter @poppyscot

The person who invented the mop must have cleaned up.

Hills. They have their ups and downs.

It's so hard to face the problem when the problem is your face.

I could do with a fizzy drink. I've been drinking coke for 5 days flat.

Follow me on twitter @poppyscot

I wanted to become a professional fisherman but I doubt I'd be able to live on the net income.

What's the worse thing about a broken calculator in a maths exam? You do the maths.

I have no time for impatient people.

Follow me on twitter @poppyscot

THANK

YOU

FOR

PURCHASING

ME!

Follow me on twitter @poppyscot

Printed in Great Britain
by Amazon.co.uk, Ltd.,
Marston Gate.